The Calm After the Storm

Dr. Deidre M. Porter

AuthorHouse™
1663 Liberty Drive
Bloomington, IN 47403
www.authorhouse.com
Phone: 833-262-8899

This book is printed on acid-free paper.

ISBN: 979-8-8230-3172-1 (sc)
979-8-8230-3173-8 (e)

Library of Congress Control Number: 2024916582

Print information available on the last page.

Published by AuthorHouse 08/22/2024

authorHOUSE®

The CALM After the STORM

Working through unsettling emotions to experience the peace of God

by

Dr. Deidre M. Porter

Illustrated by Miles Stripling

This book is dedicated in loving memory to my father,
Deacon Joe Stripling.

Thank you for always encouraging me to write and showering me with your unconditional love.
I love you and miss you dearly. RIP, Daddy-O.

Love,
Deed 🖤

Contents

How to Use this Book..ix

Introduction xi

ENVY..1

CONTENTMENT 7

FEAR 13

FAITH 19

ANGER...25

KINDNESS...31

ANXIETY 37

PEACE 43

HATRED 49

LOVE..55

SHAME...61

RESPECT 67

GUILT 73

HUMILITY 79

SADNESS...85

JOY...91

Epiphany 97

"Dad's Eulogy"..98

Acknowledgements..105

About the Author...107

Bibliography 109

How to Use this Book

In this beautiful, poetic, meditation journal, readers are invited to experience the realities of life in an artful, colorful, and majestic way. The **dark** poems in this book represent the times in our lives when we are in desolation. Whereas, the **light** poems in the book represent those moments when we are in consolation and are aware of God's presence in our lives and cognizant of His unconditional peace and love for us. Moving from desolation to consolation is aided by the act of journaling, which serves as a vehicle for readers to work through their difficulties via writing and meditation.

Introduction

In coping with life's everyday challenges and traumas, we can easily fall into patterns of negative thoughts and debilitating feelings of despair and desolation. Although this is a very authentic experience within our human existence, we need to remember that during these extremely vulnerable and difficult times in our lives, we are **not** alone. As Psalm 23: 1-4 states, "The Lord is my shepherd, I shall not want. He makes me lie down in green pastures; he leads me beside still waters; he restores my soul. He leads me in the right paths for his name's sake. Even though I walk through the darkest valley, I fear no evil; for you are with me; your rod and your staff—they comfort me."

Therefore, the next time you find yourself succumbing to a dismal state of mind or disposition, just recall God's message and promises to you. Remind yourself that the presence of God brings serenity and calm to your mind, body, and spirit every moment you are alive. So, find time to spend with Him. Listen to His voice and lean in to His everlasting peace and love.

May God bless you and your family!

ENVY

This box is empty, that door is closed;
Where's all MY stuff, all that I'm owed?

I can't envision the glass as half full;
Since I want a break, a push with NO pull.

There's no such thing as cool, rose-colored specks;
For as far as I see, there's zilch to expect.

My head is spinning while eyeing from afar;
Yep, I was so right, HE got that new car!

What will it take for ME to get one up?
My blood, sweat, and tears are just not enough.

I work so hard, yet SHE gets the big bucks;
I sure could use a stroke of HER luck!

Should I be nicer, kinder, a little less meaner?;
Ha! Who am I kidding? YOUR grass is just greener!

Lord,

Help me to see that <u>contentment</u> in my life is a direct by-product of being grateful.

_____

_____

_____

_____

_____

_____

_____

_____

_____

_____

_____

_____

_____

_____

_____

_____

_____

_____

_____

_____

_____

_____

_____

_____

_____

_____

_____

_____

_____

_____

_____

_____

Lord,

Help me to see that <u>contentment</u> in my life is a direct by-product of being grateful.

_____

_____

_____

_____

_____

_____

_____

_____

_____

_____

_____

_____

_____

_____

_____

_____

Psalm 16:11

"You show me the path of life. In your presence there is fullness of joy;
in your right hand are pleasures forevermore."

CONTENTMENT

I'm happy with me AND happy with you;
We're in this together to create something new.

Where I am now is a testament to God's grace;
For the scars from my past don't show upon my face.

It's not a perfect world I know, this I must accept;
I just put one foot forward and let God's hands do the rest.

What are my gifts to add to this amazing atmosphere?
I'm answering my own question now: "Why was I put here?"

Regardless of the shape I'm in, there's still a job to do;
Understanding my true purpose is my greatest clue.

Soaking the seeds planted for me in my garden of life;
Hasn't been without its share of grief, anguish, and strife.

But, if I keep my eyes so fixed on the prize above;
One day I'll have eternity to spend with those I love.

Contentment is—

_____

_____

_____

_____

_____

_____

_____

_____

_____

_____

_____

_____

_____

_____

_____

_____

Contentment is—

_____

_____

_____

_____

_____

_____

_____

_____

_____

_____

_____

_____

_____

FEAR

What began so innocent from loud noises and falling;
Grew something so massive and simply quite appalling.

No sleeping, no eating, no playing, or mingling;
Just grabbing for stuff and all that is blinging.

Hoarding and shoving are habits quick to form;
Expecting the unexpected is now my new norm.

Rash decisions, hasty actions, and days moving fast;
Clear visions, rational thoughts are things of the past.

Overwhelmed with what-ifs, uncertainty, and delusion;
Chaos, my accomplice, creates more confusion.

My reliable sixth sense isn't making a peep;
My insight and compass have checked out to sleep.

Make the twirling stop so my feet touch the ground;
Paralyzed in time on this doomed merry-go-round.

Lord,

Increase my <u>faith</u> in You and Your promises.

_____

_____

_____

_____

_____

_____

_____

_____

_____

_____

_____

_____

_____

_____

_____

Lord,

Increase my <u>faith</u> in You and Your promises.

_____

_____

_____

_____

_____

_____

_____

_____

_____

_____

_____

_____

_____

_____

Psalm 46:10

"Be still, and know that I am God!
I am exalted among the nations,
I am exalted in the earth."

FAITH[1]

I said, "Lord, but wait—I cannot see";
He replied, "I am your eyes— just keep following Me."

Faith is the unawareness of where you are going;
It's following God blindly because He is all-knowing.

He'll only lead you down paths of true healing;
But He is not pushy—you must be willing.

For in God's hands everything you fear is dissolved;
Your pain and your sorrow will all be resolved.

So, let go and let God—it's the right thing to do;
And you'll be amazed at how He'll help you through.

---

[1] Porter, D. M. (2011). Faith. In *Ten Poems of Healing* (pp. 79). Poem, AuthorHouse.

Faith is—

_____

_____

_____

_____

_____

_____

_____

_____

_____

_____

_____

_____

_____

_____

Faith is—

_____

_____

_____

_____

_____

_____

_____

_____

_____

_____

_____

_____

_____

_____

_____

_____

_____

ANGER

No! I didn't deserve a response that was rude;
They are the problem with their bad attitudes.

If I smile first, you should smile too;
No need to snub 'cause I don't look like you.

I've tried to play fair and treat others right;
But this bitterness inside makes me want to fight.

When I have been dissed for no reason at all;
It's time for revenge and building my wall.

Whether intended or not, it doesn't matter to me;
If I didn't like it, my wrath you will see.

Like a flame flaring high from a candle burning low;
My emotions are unleashed without anywhere to go.

And once you're locked out, it's so hard to return;
For a hot, smoldering fire will always cause burns.

Lord,

Instill in me the desire to be <u>kind</u> to everyone who crosses my path.

_____

_____

_____

_____

_____

_____

_____

_____

_____

_____

_____

_____

_____

_____

_____

_____

_____

_____

_____

_____

_____

_____

_____

_____

_____

_____

_____

_____

_____

_____

_____

Lord,

Instill in me the desire to be <u>kind</u> to everyone who crosses my path.

_____

_____

_____

_____

_____

_____

_____

_____

_____

_____

_____

_____

_____

_____

_____

Psalm 112:5

"It is well with the man who deals generously and lends;
who conducts his affairs with justice."

KINDNESS

A greeter's arms extended, outstretched and opened wide;
Sincerely, with a genuine warmth, ushering me inside.

Her natural smile just filled me with a refreshing calm;
My apprehension subsided—no more sweaty palms.

Belonging is all we humans want to ever truly feel;
A comfortable seat at the table, enjoying a hearty meal.

We all may look quite different, having varied concerns and such;
But our sameness is what's greater and that's what matters so much.

When someone new is welcomed and treated with dignity and grace;
The behavior becomes contagious and moves throughout the whole place.

Our lives should be examples for those who watch and see;
Spreading good will and good fortune, owning our true decree.

One act of sheer benevolence can cause a chain reaction;
Since God will always share with us His love and satisfaction.

Kindness is—

_____

_____

_____

_____

_____

_____

_____

_____

_____

_____

_____

_____

_____

_____

_____

_____

Kindness is—

_____

_____

_____

_____

_____

_____

_____

_____

_____

_____

_____

_____

_____

_____

_____

_____

ANXIETY

My nerves are still shot when things *are* going right;
For what this might mean is peril's in sight.

Thoughts of calamity and all the worse cases;
Shatter my peace and take me to dark places.

I wish I had faith and someone to trust;
This world can be crazy, a guide is a must.

Most days I just wonder when the other shoe will drop;
Never minding the present and all that I've got.

Will I ever be grateful and not worry so much?
Or will I need nets and buoys to clutch?

Danger's always lurking, it's planning a sneak attack;
Too nervous and frightened, to know God's got my back.

It's exhausting to believe in just what I see;
For all that's revealed is, "Oh, woe is me!"

Lord,

Reveal to me how true <u>peace</u> only comes from You.

_____

_____

_____

_____

_____

_____

_____

_____

_____

_____

_____

_____

_____

_____

Lord,

Reveal to me how true <u>peace</u> only comes from You.

_____

_____

_____

_____

_____

_____

_____

_____

_____

_____

_____

_____

_____

_____

_____

Psalm 119:165

"Great peace have those who love your law;
nothing can make them stumble."

PEACE[2]

Serenity and calmness are both attributes of peace;
It's the feeling of tranquility from your head to your feet.

It's not being worried about the inevitable or other concerns;
It's turning matters over to God—that's what we have learned.

To capture peace in our lives is like winning the Nobel Prize;
For it's in this state of mind that our strength is realized.

The wisdom to know what we can and can't change;
Is a marvelous revelation—a healthy exchange.

For these feelings of peace will continue to flow;
Because God holds the reins when we let them go.

---

[2] Porter, D. M. (2011). Peace. In *Ten Poems of Healing* (pp. 71). Poem, AuthorHouse.

Peace is—

_____

_____

_____

_____

_____

_____

_____

_____

_____

_____

_____

_____

_____

_____

_____

_____

_____

Peace is—

_____

_____

_____

_____

_____

_____

_____

_____

_____

_____

_____

_____

_____

_____

_____

_____

HATRED

Cancer is sickening, but you make me sicker;
The mere sight of your face is one instant trigger.

If I could be ruler for only a day;
One demand I would make is to send you away.

Seeing you well, or even doing great;
Makes my skin crawl, and alters my state.

Feeling such disdain for things I can't control;
Knowing someone I loved is now someone I loathe.

Or, maybe you're an outsider, a stranger I see;
Someone unknown, but still threatening to me.

My ire seems pent, my sentiments seem real;
Is this my own bias to mask what I feel?

Others keep saying, "Move on," "Turn the page";
But I'm stuck in quicksand, and inside my rage.

Lord,

Give me the grace to <u>love</u> others unconditionally as You <u>love</u> me.

_____

_____

_____

_____

_____

_____

_____

_____

_____

_____

_____

_____

_____

_____

_____

_____

_____

_____

_____

_____

_____

_____

_____

_____

_____

_____

_____

_____

_____

_____

Lord,

Give me the grace to <u>love</u> others unconditionally as You <u>love</u> me.

Psalm 85:10

"Steadfast love and faithfulness will meet;
righteousness and peace will kiss each other."

LOVE[3]

Have you ever loved someone so much that it hurt?
The thoughts of this person were constant—at rest and at work.

When he/she felt feelings— you felt the same ones too;
Whenever desires arose you knew just what to do.

You were in sync in everything—in all that you did;
Before either of you spoke—you knew what would be said.

True love feels timeless continuing without ceasing;
You would be hard pressed to find anything more pleasing.

True love is unselfish, unyielding and kind;
It's having the other's best interest in mind.

But for true love to remain in its purest of form;
Something else needs to happen that changes the norm.

It's God—He must be present in this relationship too;
After all, He sustains the love and all that you do.

---

[3] Porter, D. M. (2011). Love. In *Ten Poems of Healing* (pp. 63). Poem, AuthorHouse.

Love is—

_____

_____

_____

_____

_____

_____

_____

_____

_____

_____

_____

_____

_____

Love is—

_____

_____

_____

_____

_____

_____

_____

_____

_____

_____

_____

_____

_____

_____

_____

SHAME

Everyone knows, everyone sees;
Someone to blame, the scapegoat is me.

Don't look at my face 'cause I'm not really here;
My eyes are enshrouded, overshadowed by tears.

I can't see you, so you don't exist;
Isolated from judgment, alone in my midst.

Blaring like sirens are my shortfalls and flaws;
Humiliation cuts deep like tigers with claws.

Labeled stupid and dumb are recurring events;
I'm avoiding all criticism to any extent.

I'm fraught with timidity and insecure feelings;
Will people find out the junk I'm concealing?

Mistakes have been made, now it's my time to hide;
Consumed with self-doubt and stripped of my pride.

Lord,

Increase the <u>respect</u> I show myself and others as I search for You in all things.

_____

_____

_____

_____

_____

_____

_____

_____

_____

_____

_____

_____

_____

_____

Lord,

Increase the <u>respect</u> I show myself and others as I search for You in all things.

_____

_____

_____

_____

_____

_____

_____

_____

_____

_____

_____

_____

_____

_____

_____

_____

Psalm 15:1-3

"O Lord, who may abide in your tent? Who may dwell on your holy hill? Those who walk blamelessly, and do what is right, and speak the truth from their heart; who do not slander with their tongue, and do no evil to their friends, nor take up a reproach against their neighbors."

RESPECT

I do see you—all of you—standing before my eyes;
But, to appreciate your true essence, I must know what's inside.

Just as God has formed me in every special way;
His artistry's seen again and again in those I meet each day.

Loving myself is the beginning phase, which allows me to love another;
Instead of a stranger I now see the face of my own brother.

How do I want to be treated by all? I rhetorically ask;
Putting myself in someone else's shoes will easily accomplish this task.

Since I'm not nearly perfect and mistakes seem to be retold;
The grace I show when others do fail, God gives me ten-fold.

Always taking the high road and repeating all the steps;
Isn't a simple mission, but is worthy of all the reps.

Esteeming those I encounter is a worthwhile goal;
Noticing God in others is what enriches my soul.

Respect is—

_____

_____

_____

_____

_____

_____

_____

_____

_____

_____

_____

_____

_____

_____

_____

_____

Respect is—

_____

_____

_____

_____

_____

_____

_____

_____

_____

_____

_____

_____

_____

_____

GUILT

Playing the tape, once again in my head;
It's ruined for sure, the friendship is dead.

My wants and desires took me for a ride;
Nothing else really mattered, until later I cried.

After ego-centric motives grabbed a hold of my mind;
I was full of regret and tried to rewind.

But, too late for sorries, apologies and such;
Damage is done—the hurt was too much.

Must live with myself, the heartaches and pain;
Unworthiness and fault, keep calling my name.

Seeking pardon from peers for betrayal of trust;
Not sure that resolves my endless disgust.

Embarrassed, abashed, and quite disgraced too;
Can't forgive myself now—so what's left to do?

Lord,

Help me see that my <u>humility</u> is Your presence within me.

_____

_____

_____

_____

_____

_____

_____

_____

_____

_____

_____

_____

_____

_____

Lord,

Help me see that my <u>humility</u> is Your presence within me.

_____

_____

_____

_____

_____

_____

_____

_____

_____

_____

_____

_____

_____

_____

Psalm 25:9

"He leads the humble in what is right, and teaches the humble his way."

HUMILITY

Self-love is hard to come by when my vices can be observed;
But, God's sincere compassion supplies more than what I deserve.

These treasures that I've been granted come with no strings attached;
When sharing them with others, God's goodness goes unmatched.

Forgiveness that I've bestowed myself, I can extend to foes;
Knowing that I am loved by God is the only way this flows.

During times of stress and painfulness, I feel so tightly wound;
Then gratitude peeks through my shades, spews blessings all around.

Recalling all the favor received, can be my daily routine;
I'll discover my own blind spots and anything lost in between.

When life seems dark and dreary, gray clouds stay in one mass;
I'll remember that all is never lost because this too shall pass.

If my heart stays modest, while searching for God's truths;
I'll be a good companion to those who seek Him too.

Humility is—

_____
_____
_____
_____
_____
_____
_____
_____
_____
_____
_____
_____
_____
_____
_____
_____

_____

_____

_____

_____

_____

_____

_____

_____

_____

_____

_____

_____

_____

_____

_____

Humility is—

_____

_____

_____

_____

_____

_____

_____

_____

_____

_____

_____

_____

_____

_____

_____

SADNESS

To love and to lose, is a rite that's for sure;
A path often traveled, a road we endure.

Loving is easy, but loss is what stings;
No one gets one without the other it seems.

Hearts truly broken, have a fracture that's real;
Lifelines clearly siphoned, a pain we can feel.

Misery and sorrow are two unwanted foes;
Whose kiss is predetermined during hardships and lows.

Bounded and constricted by pressure it bears;
Fighting for freedom from all life's despair.

Distress and grief posture doom and gloom;
Darkness and fog hover the soul-less tomb.

Anguish and mourning, never averted by fate;
Weight of the world, a route we can't escape.

Lord,

Open my heart to experience <u>joy</u> in my everyday life.

_____

_____

_____

_____

_____

_____

_____

_____

_____

_____

_____

_____

_____

_____

_____

_____

Lord,

Open my heart to experience joy in my everyday life.

_____

_____

_____

_____

_____

_____

_____

_____

_____

_____

_____

_____

_____

_____

Psalm 30:11-12

"You have turned
my mourning into dancing;
you have taken off my sackcloth
and clothed me with joy,
so that my soul may praise you
and not be silent.
O Lord my God,
I will give thanks to you forever."

JOY

Unbridled bliss coming from deep, isn't a one of a kind;
It's added to and multiplied through via our state of mind.

Gratefulness and patience are igniters of these dreams;
Having buds of hope and faith are all we really need.

Overflowing in abundance when choosing what's right from wrong;
Magnanimity becomes a staple when others are brought along.

Manufactured from always ceding and never taking too much;
A gift that keeps on giving similar to the Midas touch.

Life's common imperfections don't seem to stop its bursts;
Dutifully bringing succor to anything that hurts.

Focusing on the pluses and all that goes as planned;
Elevates our endorphins and increases our life-span.

Thank You Lord for giving us life, light, and You;
Promising to praise You more in all we say and do.

Joy is—

_____

_____

_____

_____

_____

_____

_____

_____

_____

_____

_____

_____

_____

_____

_____

Joy is—

_____

_____

_____

_____

_____

_____

_____

_____

_____

_____

_____

_____

_____

_____

_____

_____

_____

Epiphany

I have come to realize that I was extremely blessed to have had a father who reminded me a lot of Jesus when He was on earth. I remember trying to capture my father's fervent spirit when writing his eulogy in December 2016. At his funeral Mass, the church was standing room only and every ethnicity and walk of life you can imagine was represented in the congregation. It felt like a little slice of heaven! Each day that passes by, I constantly strive to become more like him. In sharing his eulogy with you, I hope you get a glimpse of his unwavering obedience when answering God's call. In addition, I pray that you are inspired by him to continue your own life's journey with courage, compassion, joy, and love. ♥

"Dad's Eulogy"

Good Morning, Everyone!

On Tuesday, I was talking to my daughter, Rikki, over the phone (she was away at college) and she said, "Mom, I forgot to tell you—on Sunday after you told me that Grandpa had passed away, I went to mass at the church near the ocean and the priest gave one of the best homilies that I have ever heard." I said, "Really?!? What did he say?" She continued, "He said, 'Do you know how on every tombstone there is the date that the person was born, a dash in the middle, then the date that the person died?' He said, 'The most important part of it all is the dash in the middle! That is because the dash in the middle represents how that person lived his/her life while here on earth. For example, did that person live a life that was pleasing to God?' He went on to say that we can live a life that is pleasing to God by treating everyone we encounter with love, compassion, and mercy." After our conversation was over, I thought to myself, Yes! That's it—Dad was a person who treated everyone he met with love, compassion, and mercy.

I remember many times, walking with my dad through the church parking lot and parishioners would see him from afar and they would begin smiling and waving so vigorously. I thought, WOW! They were so excited to see him as if he were a celebrity! I truly believe people loved being in my dad's presence because he brought them so much JOY. He made them feel good about themselves AND— He always brought out the BEST in everyone, because he always looked for the BEST in everyone.

My siblings and I created a list of words we thought accurately described our dad. I will share some of them with you: Loving, Humble, Generous, Dependable, Committed, Inspiring, Truthful, Gracious, Determined, Passionate, Non-Judgmental, Intelligent, Adventurous, Faithful, Intuitive, Fun-loving, Courageous, Strong, and Loyal. When you think about him, I am certain these words resonate with you too.

However, if I had to sum up all of these characteristics into one description, I would say that my dad was a man whose dash in the middle represented something extraordinarily wonderful and definitely pleasing to God, because he embraced his vocation in life with 110% joy, effort, and love. I am not just referring to his vocation as a deacon, but also his vocation as a loving and faithful husband to my mom for 56 years; his vocation as a loving and devoted father and grandfather to his children and grandchildren; and his vocation as a loving, compassionate, loyal son, brother, brother-in-law, uncle, father-in-law, godfather, cousin, and friend to all of you. You see—he truly committed his life to all of us. I believe God said, "Joe, I need you to be a servant to my people." With enthusiasm he replied, "Yes, Lord, I will do it!"

So, as we go forth this day, let us all try to emulate my dad in our everyday lives. Whatever our vocation may be, let us live it and embrace it with 110% joy, effort, and love just as he did. In this way, we will surely keep Deacon Joe Stripling in our hearts forever. Amen!

Acknowledgements

To God my Lord and Savior, who is so merciful, kind, and generous.

To my beautiful daughter, Rikki, who undeniably fills my life with so much joy.

To my phenomenal parents Joe and Dolores Stripling, who have immeasurably blessed me with their unconditional love and faith in God (RIP, Dad).

To my exceptionally gifted and remarkably compassionate siblings, who are as talented as they are loving and caring (RIP, Marla and Erica).

To *all* my family members (both near and far), whom I love so deeply and genuinely. Thanks to each of you for being such a significant person and influence in my life.

To all my friends, who leave me speechless. I am convinced that God has selected only the best ones for me—each one of you is so very special.

To all my angels in heaven, who pray for me daily—I love you and appreciate you (RIP, Rich).

About the Author

Dr. Deidre M. Porter earned her Doctorate degree in Education with an emphasis in Educational Psychology from the University of Southern California, Master's of Arts degree in Counseling from Loyola Marymount University, and Bachelor's of Arts degree in Psychology from the University of California, Irvine. She recently retired from her rewarding career in higher education, which spanned over three decades. She was inspired to write **The Calm After the Storm** as a follow up to her seminal work, **Ten Poems of Healing**. She currently resides in Fountain Valley, California. She enjoys reading, outdoor activities, church gatherings, watching all sports, and spending as much time as possible traveling with her family and friends.

Bibliography

Porter, D. M. (2011b). Ten Poems of Healing. AuthorHouse.

Holy Bible (Catholic Edition). (1990). (Vol. The New Revised Standard Version). Oxford University Press.

Printed in the United States
by Baker & Taylor Publisher Services